Lithium & Tea

Amy Perez

MS

Psychology

Table of Contents

1

Introduction

Bipolar disorder can feel like the end of the world. There, I said it. Getting this diagnosis can feel like getting hit by a ton of bricks. I was diagnosed with bipolar disorder over a decade ago. Not a day goes by that I don't deal with some sort of battle revolving around my diagnosis. However, I won't let it stop me from living a productive life. Every day, I push through the highs and lows.

My nightstand next to my bed is full of bottles of pills from mood stabilizers to some used for sleep. Unfortunately, the chemicals in my brain do not function properly without some help. From medication to therapy and even exercise, I have a plethora of tools to ensure I live a full life even though I have bipolar disorder.

If you are in this book, you may have been diagnosed with bipolar disorder or have a loved one who has received this diagnosis. The struggle can feel like a difficult uphill battle. Many times, when I have this illness all figured out, I will be blind-sided by something new.

Each day, I learn something new when it comes to bipolar disorder. A couple of years ago, I decided to start writing about the issues I face with this mental illness. Now, I run support groups and work daily as an author and mental health advocate.

Struggling with bipolar disorder means that every day is different. One day we can move mountains and the next day it is a battle just to get out of bed. There are always surprises when it comes to this illness. In this book, we will use my master's degree in psychology to go over different topics when it comes to bipolar disorder.

Our world is forever changing. It can be difficult to handle life when it comes to battling a mental illness. There are triggers, major life changes and stress to deal with on a daily basis. Many of us have full or part-time jobs, family and many responsibilities. One thing to note is that mental illness does not discriminate. People from all walks of life have been diagnosed with bipolar disorder. Millions of people around the globe have received this diagnosis.

When I was in my early twenties, I received a diagnosis of bipolar disorder. I have had bipolar disorder in my family since birth. I was always wondering if I would develop bipolar disorder when I was a teenager. However, once I reached my twenties, I thought I was in the clear. Even though bipolar disorder runs in my family, I thought I had dodged a bullet and that I would never battle with this illness.

I was in college working towards a bachelor's degree. I met the love of my life and we decided on marriage and children and we didn't mind which one came first. Within a little over a year, we had a sweet little baby and a wedding in the works. Life was as perfect as it could have been.

I was working part-time, going to school and caring for my young baby. Life felt stressful at times, but I was handling it quite well. However, I wasn't taking the best care of myself. The next thing I knew, I laid down on the couch only to not wake up.

My then fiancé, panicked when he saw me lying there in a heap on the couch. He called an emergency line. The ambulance came and was able to revive me. I was breathing in an ammonia inhalant under my nose. I was lying on the carpet in our two-bedroom apartment.

The emergency workers put me on a stretcher and carried me out of the door. I remember the Florida sun hitting my face and then everything went dark. I woke up in an emergency room. I was told that I was low on potassium. I had a needle in my arm and hospital workers were busily coming in and out of the room.

Once I was stable, I was able to get visitors. My then fiancé came in and we were so happy to see each other. However, I just didn't feel quite right. Then, all of the sudden, my body started to shake uncontrollably.

My fiancé was kicked out of the hospital room as nurses surrounded my bed. We later learned that I was having a psychotic seizure.

I spent a couple of days in the hospital. I was in and out mentally. The next thing I knew, I woke up in an ambulance. A woman was smiling down on me. We ended up stopping behind a small building surrounded by fencing. Two men came to the ambulance to get me.

Confusion washed over my body as I was led inside the building. I was brought to a desk where a woman tried to take down my information. But by this time, I was hysterical and beyond confused. The people I was met with took my necklace along with my engagement ring and placed them in a brown envelope.

My brain was circling around in a psychosis. To read more on my experiences with different mental health facilities and my psychosis, read *Manic Episode Series*. It is available through *Amazon, Audible &* *iTunes*. However, in this book, we will take countless topics related to bipolar disorder. I will use my education and experience to usher through this book.

It is interesting to note that I wasn't diagnosed with bipolar disorder right away. My first diagnosis was post partem depression with psychotic features. It was assumed that it was a small bump in the road, and we would get through it.

Unfortunately, I missed our wedding because the place I was brought to was a mental health facility and I had to stay there until I was deemed able to go home. Even though this was my first experience with a mental health facility, it wouldn't be my last. It always seemed that each time would be more difficult than the last both mentally and physically.

Unfortunately, there is a lot of suffering when it comes to bipolar disorder. However, there is hope. Not only can we live a full life with purpose, but we can thrive in our daily life. As an author, wife and mother of two, I can assure you that we can get through a bipolar disorder diagnosis using an array of tools from therapy to self-care. Next, let's dive right in to learn about different types of bipolar disorder, let's go!

2

Types of Bipolar Disorder

The first step anyone should take when it comes to bipolar disorder is to get properly diagnosed. We always want to be open and honest with our doctor and medical support team. This can help immensely with getting a correct diagnosis. When I was first hospitalized for mental health, I literally barely said a word. I was in a major depressive episode.

Also, there was some psychosis involved.

Although mental illness runs in my family, it was all new to me as I was going through it. I was extremely confused and distraught. I didn't know where I was or what was happening. My brain found it hard to process my reality of being locked away in a mental health facility. I often wonder if I was better educated at the time, if it would have been easier.

Now I know that millions of people around the globe face issues where mental health is involved. We are never alone with the battles we face. There is always hope and someone to turn to. Personally, I know how lonely it can feel when we are at the low end with bipolar disorder. However, the highs can feel euphoric.

With that, let's go over some different types of bipolar disorder:

- Bipolar Disorder Type 1
- Bipolar Disorder Type 2
- Cyclothymic Disorder
- Mixed Features
- Rapid Cycling

It may be hard to process the different types of bipolar disorder when we are very depressed or at the very high end of the disorder. When we reach stability, it is a great time to get educated. We can take a look and learn what our triggers are and how to set boundaries. I go over that extensively in *Bipolar Disorder: Thriving, Triggers, Love and Relationships*. This book is available through *Amazon, Audible & iTunes*.

Bipolar disorder type 1 is considered to be more severe than the other types. With this type, there will be periods of mania as well as periods of depression. A general term for bipolar disorder type 1 is manic depression. Some people may wonder; who is at risk when it comes to bipolar disorder type 1? Well, according to *Web MD,* almost six million people in the United States alone have bipolar disorder type 1.

When someone has a person with bipolar disorder in their family, they are at a higher risk of developing this disorder. For me, I have two people in my immediate family with the disorder. For the biggest part of my life, I was always on the outside looking in when it comes to this illness. It wasn't until my early twenties that I started the uphill battle with bipolar disorder.

According to *Web MD,* most people are in their teens or early twenties when symptoms of bipolar disorder first appear. Before I got diagnosed, I thought I was in the clear. I had made it to age twenty-three without showing any signs or symptoms. Sure, I had highs and lows but nothing out of the ordinary.

Now let's take a look at symptoms of mania that will be present during a manic episode:

- Inflated self-image
- Rapid or pressured speech
- Going quickly from one idea to another
- Increased energy
- Hyperactivity
- Decreased need for sleep

- Excessive spending
- Hypersexuality
- Substance abuse

I can say that as a person with bipolar disorder type 1, I have battled with all of these symptoms. A person in a manic episode can pursue grandiose and even unrealistic plans as well. I have been lucky enough a few times to catch a manic episode as it's starting but other times, it will be out if my hands.

When my manic episodes reach too high, I have no choice but to go into the hospital. Once there, a team of experts can keep an eye on my and evaluate my condition. There is no shame in admitting that bipolar disorder is often bigger than the person who has it. I have found myself at the mercy of doctors, nurses and medical staff a few times.

Going into mania can be severely taxing on my brain and body. As much as I try my best to prevent it, sometimes it is out of my hands. I have learned that therapy, medicinal therapy and a reduction of stress can help to prevent a manic episode.

On the opposite side of mania is depression which can be as equally difficult. Sometimes, there are early warning signs of depression for me but sometimes it can seem to come out of nowhere. I will just feel as though I hit a brick wall. Here are some signs of the depression side of bipolar disorder:

- Feeling sad, worried or empty
- Having little to no energy
- Sleeping too little or too much
- Eating too little or too much
- Having a hard time making decisions
- Suicidal thoughts

The most important thing to note about depression is that if there are thoughts about suicide to reach out to an emergency line right away. There is nothing to be ashamed of if we are feeling suicidal. I have gone through the suicidal thinking and ideology years ago. I just remember not wanting to live despite the fact that my life was going well. Probably one of the best feelings with bipolar disorder is when a depression episode breaks, and we start to feel better.

Now, let's touch on bipolar disorder type 2. With this type, there will be an absence of mania. Those of us with bipolar disorder type 2 will have a mixture of hypomania and depression. Sometimes there can be a pattern of highs and lows while sometimes there is not. However, the trademark of bipolar disorder type 2 is the lack of mania as is present in bipolar disorder type 1.

Another difference between the two disorders is that with bipolar disorder type 2, there tends to be more depression episodes. It is good to note that people with bipolar disorder type 2 can lead a normal life just as with people with bipolar disorder type 1. Always remember, there are millions of us around the globe that have bipolar disorder.

Hypomanic symptoms are the trademark of bipolar disorder type 2. As with mania, hypomania can get us into some trouble as well. Someone who is hypomanic can be described as being the life of the party. Hypomania can give us an ability to have a great mood. This can be infectious to those around us. Now let's take a deeper look at the signs and symptoms of bipolar disorder. We will go over that next!

3

Signs & Symptoms

With bipolar disorder, we can experience extreme lows or extreme highs. Also, we can have any symptom in between. It is good to note that human beings are like snowflakes; we are all different. For instance, my experience with bipolar disorder will most likely be different than other people's. However, there are many signs and symptoms involved with bipolar disorder that are common amongst all people with this diagnosis.

It is considered that a person with bipolar disorder will experience three or more of the symptoms. This is why it is important to tell our health professionals how we are truly feeling. For me, the first sign that I am headed towards hypomania or mania is a decreased need for sleep. I will find it extremely hard to fall asleep. One piece of advice I received when it comes to sleep, is to go to sleep on the same day you wake up.

Another sign that hypomania or mania is coming is pressured speech. Those of us with bipolar disorder may talk rapidly and not allow interruption. Sometimes the words will not make sense. I have been at this place and was able to correct it without hospitalization. My husband was able to get me a visit with my doctor just in time.

Once we were with my doctor, a nurse performed an electrocardiogram. Once my doctor looked at the results, he was able to prescribe me a mood stabilizer. Also, I was given an anxiety medication which helped to calm me down. At the time, I was triggered by holiday stress and an upcoming trip. I go over triggers more in depth in: *Bipolar Disorder: Triggers Boundaries and*

Roadblocks. This book is available through *Amazon, Audible & iTunes*.

As someone with bipolar disorder, we can experience highs and lows even on the same day. Years ago, I was only taking an antipsychotic medication. However, I was having mood swings. During the first half of the day, I was lower and more negative. After a few hours, like a switch, I would feel happier and more euphoric. This went on for months until it was addressed properly.

This happened to be during the time I was in the middle of a master's degree in psychology. I was learning about bipolar disorder and with that, I learned about mood stabilizers. Once I came to my doctor, we got on the right path with medication.

Depression can hit hard when it comes to bipolar disorder. Through experience, I have found that many people in my life understand this part of the illness better. When I describe mania and what happens along with triggers, it seems hard for some people to understand. A common question can be, "What do you mean you can be too happy?"

I still battle with the idea of mania. But with the depression side, there is a separate list of signs and symptoms from fatigue, overeating and even suicidal thoughts and ideation. I would like to mention again that it is of utmost importance that if you or a loved one experiences suicidal thoughts or actions, to contact an emergency line immediately. There are trained professionals to help with this sign of bipolar disorder.

It can be hard to admit that having bipolar disorder is larger than ourselves, family and loved ones. One if my very good friends offered for me to stay with her if I ever experience a manic stage. However, if I am too far gone with mania, I will need care from trained professionals.

There could be triggers that are too much for me to handle alone or I may need a medication adjustment.

Now, let's turn to The *Mayo Clinic* for their list of signs and symptoms as well as criteria for bipolar disorder. With bipolar disorder type 1, there must be at least one manic episode that can be followed by a major depressive episode. There can even be a break from reality or a psychosis.

When it comes to bipolar disorder type 2, there will be one major depressive episode along with a hypomanic episode. As mentioned earlier, the difference between bipolar disorder type one and two is the lack of mania in type two.

When it comes to cyclothymic disorder, a person will have many periods of hypomania and depression symptoms back-to-back. It is important to note that the depression in cyclothymic disorder will be less severe than with an episode of major depression.

Mayo Clinic warns those of us with bipolar disorder to pay attention to the warning signs of bipolar disorder. It is important to keep track of triggers and not to ignore early warning signs. With my situation, I was lucky enough to prevent an episode once I learned my early signs and symptoms. As someone with bipolar disorder, we can have friends and loved ones that we can turn to in a time of crisis or if we just need to talk.

However, nothing can compare to getting help from a professional. As someone with this disorder, we need to seek medical attention during a time of crisis. I have been with my doctor fir many years. He knows me quite well and we have a great working relationship.

Like many people, I was triggered by the pandemic of the year

2020. The stress caused me to relapse with my bipolar disorder. I wasn't expecting it because I had already faced so many triggers when it comes to my mental illness. I ended up going for a stay in my local mental health hospital. Once there, my doctor called them to recommend that I take lithium three times a day.

According to The *Mayo Clinic,* there isn't really a sure-fire way to prevent a relapse with bipolar disorder. However, learning our early warning signs and symptoms can prevent our disorder from getting worse. Some of us may experience other disorders along with having bipolar disorder such as anxiety, eating disorders, battling with drugs or alcohol and even physical health problems.

This is referred to as comorbidity. Comorbidity is the simultaneous presence of two or more disease or medical conditions in one person. This can be hard to handle a as the patient as well as the health professional.

Before moving on to going further into mania in more depth, let's list out some common symptoms with mania and depression:

Mania:

- Abnormally upbeat
- Increased activity
- Agitation
- Exaggerated sense of well-being and self-confidence

Depression:

- Feeling sad, empty or hopeless
- Either insomnia or sleeping too much
- Fatigue or loss of energy

These symptoms can be taxing on our brains and bodies. Just know that we are never alone in this illness. Millions of people worldwide have received this diagnosis of bipolar disorder. Now let's go further in depth with mania.

4

Mania

As is with bipolar disorder, everyone can experience mania differently. Personally, mania puts my brain in a disabled state. I am unable to function normally. I will need medical intervention if I get to this point. According to the *Mayo Clinic,* mania and hypomania are two different things. Mania will be more severe than hypomania.

Where someone experiences hypomania, it may be noticeable at school or at work. What can happen with mania is that there can be a psychosis. When it comes to mania and hypomania, I have experienced both. Hypomania seems to be a little more manageable than mania.

For the sake of this chapter, we will take information form *Very Well Mind*. A manic episode is apparent when there is an elevated mood or even an irritable one. A person who is experiencing mania will have intense energy, racing thoughts and/or other behaviors that are extreme or exaggerated. When someone is in mania, they can even experience a psychosis. During a psychosis, a person can hallucinate, experience delusions and can altogether have a break from reality.

Here are some of the symptoms that we will go over in more detail:

- Decreased need for sleep
- Engagement in many activities
- Pressured speech
- Easily distracted
- Hypersexuality
- Increase in risky behavior
- Rapid thinking
- Flight of ideas
- Grandiosity
- Hostility
- Thoughts of suicide

- Excessive religious ideation
- Bright clothing
-

Sleep problems can be a trademark sign that mania is upon someone. When someone is manic, they will have a decreased need for sleep. This is one of the symptoms that I will experience right away. I will give myself about thirty minutes to fall asleep on my own. Then, I will turn to different sleep regimens that I use. When we are having sleep problems, this is when we need to bring it up to our healthcare provider. We could possibly avoid a manic episode.

Another sign of mania is being engaged in multiple activities at once. There can be a burst of productivity that is abnormal for the person. Also, a person approaching a manic episode or in one can have pressured speech. This can be accompanied by speaking loudly or rapidly. This will be a clear deviation from a person's normal speech.

A person who is in mania can have an increased desire for sex. This can happen to someone who is hypomanic or manic. According to *Very Well Mind*, this can be accompanied by uncharacteristic or risky sexual behavior. This could include an increased activity or sexual interactions either in person or online.

Additionally, a person who experiences mania may take on more risky behaviors. This can be in the form of overspending, spending sprees and even gambling. For this reason, personally, I will separate money into accounts that I would not be able to immediately use. Also, leaving credit cards at home while out shopping can help with overspending.

Another trademark of bipolar disorder mania can be rapid thinking. A person could appear to be talking normally but, on the inside, they are very troubled with rapid thinking. Also, it is good to take notice if there is a presence of a flight of ideas. This can be apparent when it is hard to make logical sense of the progression of a discussion. This will be obvious if a person jumps from one idea to another without the topics being related.

A symptom that is also present in mania but not typically in hypomania is grandiosity. A person who experiences feelings of grandiosity can have delusions of grandeur. A person experiencing this symptom can think that they are famous or that they are connected with someone who is.

Another symptom of bipolar disorder mania is irritability. Everyone can get irritable from time to time. However, this will be an abnormal amount of irritability or even hostility.

In order for a person to receive a diagnosis or mania, they will need to experience it for at least one week. Also, there will need to be three or more of the symptoms listed previously present. According to *Very Well Mind*, there is no cure for manic episodes. A person may need medication, therapy and even lifestyle changes in order to manage having bipolar disorder.

Mania can be treated immediately with an antipsychotic but a medication that would be more long-term would be a mood stabilizer. A mood stabilizer can help prevent any future episodes. Along with a mood stabilizer and an antipsychotic, a person can be prescribed a medication used for sleep as well.

The last time I experienced mania was at the beginning of the recent pandemic. I ended up being hospitalized for a few weeks. After being observed, I was eventually given lithium as a mood stabilizer.

Also, the hospital used Zyprexa as an antipsychotic. It is a hard realization that mania can come when we least expect it.

Personally, when I experience mania, I am heartbroken because my loved ones and friends suffer with me. It disrupts my life as well as the life of those around me. Going into mania effects my relationships, work life and sometimes even finances. After my most recent bout of mania, I was able to start therapy. We used telecommunication due to the pandemic, but it helped a lot.

My therapist asked me many challenging questions and was there to listen to what I had to say. I would highly recommend going through therapy whether there is a bipolar disorder diagnosis or not. During therapy, moods can be identified along with triggers.

Going through a manic episode can be tragic for the individual as well as for those around them. It is hard for me because as soon as I feel like I have identified all of my triggers, I am confronted with a new one. However, there are many ways that we can change our lifestyle to help prevent or manage a manic episode.

It is important to make time for exercise. Getting daily exercise can help a lot with bipolar disorder symptoms. Also, having a well-rounded diet can help us as well. We want to make sure not to skip meals. Possibly, most importantly, we want to stick to a proper sleep schedule. We want to get a full night of rest.

Next, we will look at the opposite end of the spectrum of bipolar disorder. Although the symptoms are completely opposite of mania, they can be equally debilitating.

5

Depression

It may sound odd, but I
welcome the depression side of my
bipolar disorder more than the mania.
It is usually less disabling. It's hard
though because of the lack of energy
and I want to sleep a lot. However,
there is a calmness to the depression
side. Unfortunately, depression can
slip down and create suicidal thoughts
and ideation. If you or someone you
know experiences these thoughts or
ideations, it is considered an
emergency. Make sure to call an

emergency line or go to an emergency room right away.

There are many steps we can take when it comes to bipolar depression. According to *Web MD*, in order to fight depression, we shouldn't drink alcohol or use drugs. This could make our mood worse or keep our medication from working properly. Over five years ago, I was not properly medicated. I started drinking wine at night to help me sleep. This may have worked temporarily but after some time, it exasperated my symptoms. We will go over alcohol more in depth later.

Another step with depression in bipolar disorder is to stick to a routine. We will want to go to bed and wake up at the same time each day. Also, we will want to eat meals and exercise at the same time each day. Personally, having a routine has saved me. As an author, I do the same work at the same time every day.

On the weekends, I will work slightly less than I would in a weekday. Also, I stick to a rule of writing one chapter a day on the days that I work. I will take my medication and eat breakfast at the same time each day. On the weekends, I will stick to the same routine.

When I am feeling the depression of bipolar disorder, I will try to go easy on myself. If I don't get everything done in one day that I wanted to get done, that's okay. One challenge I faced during the depression side is that I can be easily triggered by something negative.

For instance, someone sent me a rude message during a depressive episode. It really bothered me, and it took me a while to get over it. Had I been more stable when I got the message, it may not have bothered me as much. This is why it is so important to have a support system.

When I come across a problem, I will turn to certain friends and family for support. When I am dealing with issues, I will turn to people in my life for support. Depending on the size of the issue I face, I will depend on different people. My best friends and I will discuss my illness in great depth. I will often remind them that bipolar disorder is often times bigger than me. As much as I try to handle bipolar disorder on my own, I will always need to reach out for help.

One tip that I find helpful is not to make major life changes during a depressive episode. For those of us with bipolar disorder and those of us who do not suffer from any ailments, we will find that we are often hit with major life changes. Some are within our control and some are not.

A couple of years ago, I was hit with a major life change. My grandfather passed away. I wasn't expecting it to hit me as hard as it did. I would find myself tearing up at random times during the day. Also, small things would remind me of him and would trigger a sadness. Like my bipolar disorder, this major life change was bigger than me and I had no control over it. It is good for us to realize the symptoms of depression in bipolar disorder, which can be:

- Feeling sad, worried or empty
- Having little to no energy
- Unable to enjoy things
- Sleep too little or too much
- Having a hard time getting out of bed
- Eat too much or too little
- Trouble focusing
- Trouble remembering things
- Having a hard time making decisions
- Thoughts of suicide or death

I have read in many places and hear it as well to keep a mood journal. This way we can see how our moods can fluctuate during the day, weeks and months. For many of us, it can be hard to admit to those around us that we are depressed. Personally, I may not even notice I was depressed until it is in the past. Once I am feeling better, I will look back and see that I was very depressed.

Let's take a look at the difference between unipolar depression and bipolar disorder depression. When someone has unipolar depression, there will be depression mixed in with levels of stability or periods of not feeling as depressed. When it comes to bipolar depression, there will be periods of lows and highs.

Did you know that people with bipolar disorder will typically experience more depression than mania? There can up to three times as many depressive episodes than manic episodes. Also, the depression can last at least fifty percent longer.

There are two chemicals in the brain that impact bipolar disorder depression which are dopamine and serotonin. Dopamine can play a large role in our thoughts and emotions. Also, it can control our body movements. When we are depressed, our dopamine can be decreased. A decrease in dopamine can cause a lack of motivation and body movement. With serotonin, a decreased amount can be associated with sadness or a depressed mood.

According to *Better Help*, depressive episodes can last for weeks or even months. Those of who are suffering from a depressive episode, we will have a low level of energy and even a low mood.

Certain life events, seasons, and even age can trigger a depressive episode. Here where I live, we have long winters. Personally, I slow down in the winter months. However, I can be triggered during the holidays. I have noticed more manic episodes occurring for me when I lived in a warm, tropical climate. However, living where there are season changes, I experience less manic symptoms.

It is important that we are open and honest with those around us as well as with our medical team when it comes to our symptoms. This will help to ensure that we are properly medicated. Throughout the decade since I have been diagnosed with bipolar disorder, I have been on a few different medications.

The longest I have been hospital free was for six years. I started on Latuda and then I started on Lamictal after a few years. Also, I was diagnosed with anxiety during this time. I was given an anti-anxiety medication to take along with it. Next, we will take a look at what happens when we experience mania and depression at the same time.

6

Mixed Episodes

As if having either mania or depression at one time isn't hard enough, some of us may experience mixed episodes. This can be described as being in mania or hypomania and having three or more depressive symptoms at the same time. Also, it could be a depressive episode with three or more manic symptoms present. When this happens, it can be extremely taxing on our brains and bodies.

One of my most difficult episodes with bipolar disorder was when I had a mixed episode. It started off as higher energy and less of a need for sleep. This was about a year and a half after receiving a diagnosis of post partem depression with psychotic features. I was taking medications and then I didn't think I needed it anymore.

However, after a few short months of not having my medication, my symptoms returned, and they were worse than before. At the time, I didn't have insurance, so I had to go to my local county-ran hospital. My husband brought me there because we had nowhere else to turn.

My mixed episode happened to be mania with depression mixed in. So, I would have high energy mixed with despair and crying. It was so difficult because I couldn't control me mind, thoughts or body. When I got brought to the South *County Mental Health Facility*, in south Florida, I was in the middle of a mixed episode.

At first, I was in the front part of the hospital for observation. As I was in there, patients came and went. Police officers and ambulance workers would bring in people night and day. The hospital workers would bring us drinks and food periodically. We were offered plastic lawn chairs to sit on.

At night, there wasn't much room for us to sleep. So, mental health technicians would bring us plastic mats to sleep on. I remember being upset because the women and men were sleeping so close to each other. Because my mixed episode was mostly manic, the nurse brought me in to see the doctor. He asked me if I would like a shot to help me sleep. At this time, I was exhausted and reluctantly agreed.

I did not know it then, but the shot was called Haldol. Little did I know that I would become very familiar with this medication in the years to come. I was told to pull my pants down a bit and bend forward. The shot was given in my buttocks. I was then told to go lie down while the medication took effect.

I did as instructed. I went into the waiting room area where mats were lying on the floor. To my surprise, there was a sign on the door that read, "Girls Only". A mental health technician took in my complaint about the girls and the guys sleeping in the same space. That night, there were people lined up and down the hallway to sleep.

The Haldol worked to put me to sleep that night. I woke up in the sunny waiting room with the plastic lawn chairs in my view. After being observed, it was decided that I would stay at the *South County Mental Hospital.* A mental health technician brought me through to the double doors that led from the waiting room into the main part of the hospital.

The first thing I noticed was my name written in red on a white board with about twenty men's names. I was shocked to realize my new reality. Again, my mixed episode cam raging back in my brain. I remember a feeling of rage filled my body and brain.

Again, this illness can be bigger than any one person alone. While I wasn't too happy with my conditions, I was where I needed to be. It's a difficult reality to be stuck in a place in a mixed episode but sometimes it is necessary.

So, how is a mixed episode treated? Health professionals will administer a medication to treat the main symptoms. If we are experiencing mainly mania, we will be given an antipsychotic medication. Also, a mood stabilizer can be given. If we are experiencing mainly depression, then an antidepressant can be given.

How do we know if what we are experiencing is a mixed episode? For starters, mania and depression will occur at the same time in a rapid sequence. The two different moods can alternate or appear at the same time.

It is good to note that if we or a loved experience a mixed episode with bipolar disorder, that we are not alone. Almost three percent of the United States population has bipolar disorder. Of those millions of people, at least half of them will experience some sort of mixed symptoms.

It is interesting to note that if someone is diagnosed with bipolar disorder during their adolescence, they are more likely to experience a mixed episode. Even though someone can experience a mixed episode, they are still just as likely to have an only manic or only depression episode. According to *Web MD*, the co-occurrence of mania and depression are quite common.

So, what exactly does a mixed episode look like? A person could be crying and hysterical and then claim that they have never felt better. On the outside, a person could be jumping for joy in one instance and then fall with joy in one instance and then fall with misery. Then a little later be extremely ecstatic.

It is important to note that a mixed episode could last from days to weeks to even months if it is not treated. Therefore, it is so important to have a good medical team. Also, we will want to be open and honest with how we are feeling. This can ensure better care and faster recovery.

It is interesting to note that recovery from a mixed episode can take longer than pure depression or pure mania. According to *Web MD*, people who are experiencing a mixed episode are more likely to commit suicide than someone who is experiencing depression. It is good to note that lithium is often used during this time for someone with bipolar disorder. According to *Web MD*, if lithium is taken long-term it can reduce the risk of suicide.

Lithium has been used for bipolar disorder for over sixty years. As with many medications, it can take weeks to fully take effect. With my most recent episode, I was given lithium to take once in the day and once again at night. It was a good medication to help get rid of the manic highs and dramatic lows of the depression.

In addiction to mood stabilizers, there are many antipsychotics such as Latuda and Zyprexa which can be used in combination. These are considered to be used in order to prevent an episode. For extreme cases in bipolar disorder, electroconvulsive therapy may be used. This is also known as ECT. Next, let's dive deeper into how someone receives a diagnosis with bipolar disorder.

7

Diagnosis

The road to getting a proper diagnosis can be long, stressful and scary. Each episode I have ever had seems to be just as grueling as the ones in the past. Getting the right diagnosis can be important for getting the proper care, medication and even health insurance. If you or a loved one is struggling with a bipolar disorder diagnosis, just know that you are not alone.

Millions of people around the world face the ups and downs with bipolar disorder. First, I was diagnosed with post partem depression with psychotic features. Dealing with psychosis was extremely challenging. Nothing could have prepared me for the first episode I experienced.

In *Manic Episode Series,* I go through the lived experience of my psychosis. Also, I experienced different hospitals and facilities. Until I experienced the first symptoms of bipolar disorder, I knew it was in my family. Also, I had worked at countless assisted living facilities and nursing homes with a traveling doctor. Many of the patients suffered from mental health disorders. Also, many of the patients had AIDS and various ailments.

I would ride in the car with the physician all around south Florida. I was so used to writing bipolar disorder on charts that it become second nature. From my experience, so many of our patients were in really bad shape. I was extremely worried about their health and quality of life.

All I could do was to make sure that they received the best care from me while I was there. Patients would often say and do the most outlandish things. Many of them were stricken with despair. We saw young patients, elderly patients and everyone in between. They were at the mercy of government funding and the facilities that they stayed in. I have vivid memories of some of the patients. One woman begged me for one dollar to use on a vending machine.

After I got off work at that job, I would work my second job at an upscale restaurant. Most of the cliental seemed wealthy and well-off. I was always battling at the difference between the people who seemed to be wasting away in crummy assisted living facilities while others were enjoying fine wine and gourmet food.

However, once I had my first episode, my world collided with one I only experienced from the outside looking in. I was once a health care worker, helping patients with bipolar disorder. I got to go home every night and enjoy some homemade food. I could clean my apartment and take a nice hot shower. I could cuddle in my nice warm bed. I had no knowledge of what it was like to be trapped in a facility battling a mental health condition.

Then I found myself inside of a mental hospital in the middle of my first episode. I felt lost, trapped, alone and terrified. All of my comforts from home were gone. Once the door closed behind me, I was locked in with the facility's workers and my fellow patients.

We were offered merely things to barely survive. I found a room; 210. I went in and found two beds with a fluorescent light on overhead. The "bed" towards the back was merely a thin green mat. On it was a very thin pillow with no case.

There on that bed, I shed a lot of tears and worked through a lot of confusion as to why I was even there. I was losing weight by the day. I would stay up all night out of psychosis and fear and sleep during the day because it felt safer that way. A man would bang on my door every morning in order for me to get my blood pressure taken. Also, we were required to take whatever pill or pills that they gave us.

I was never one to take a lot of medicine so in my mind, even that part was scary. For some reason, I never made it to the meals. I would wake up to the smell of food. I would come out of room 210 and there would be no food to be found.

For a while, my then fiancé was my only visitor. He regularly visited me. In that facility, he was allowed to bring me food. He would bring me dishes from his mother's kitchen or a homemade sandwich. I would barely take one bite because I was so far in a psychosis. I was stricken with sadness and guilt. I kept thinking that I did something wrong or horrible to be in there.

Now that I am more aware of my bipolar disorder diagnosis, I can put my past into perspective. Before I experienced a mental health ailment, I had a strong mind. I could handle large amounts of stress. I never needed medication or monthly visits with a psychiatrist.

It took a lot of trial and error to really figure out what my specific mental health ailment is. We assumed, at first, that I just had a brush with post partem depression. I was told to only take my medications until a certain amount of time. Once we were in the clear with my depression, I was able to go off of my medication. However, within the year, another episode appeared. This time it wasn't depression with psychotic features, it was a manic episode.

Again, we were at the mercy of a mental health facility. My brain was full of confusion and fear. At this time, we knew it was something bigger than us. Also, it was out of our control until I received a proper diagnosis. My mental health team worked to get me stabilized and in a better place.

Now, my diagnosis is bipolar disorder type one. It is categorized as the more severe type. However, I found a medicinal therapy that worked for my brain. I was able to stay stable for many years. Nonetheless, if I did not receive the right diagnosis, it would have been hard to find the right treatment.

Even after receiving a high level of stability, it was important for me to take care of myself. It was important to get plenty of rest and good nutrition. It was imperative to make exercise and self-care a priority. I had to recognize my triggers and work around them or create boundaries.

Once we learn how our bipolar disorder impacts our life, we can build our world towards stability and happiness. My goal is to stay stable and out of the hospital but sometimes the hospital is the best place to be. Now that I have better insurance, I can go to different hospitals that are ran in a different way. I will forever be grateful to the mental health workers that have seen me through this journey of getting a proper diagnosis.

8

Psychosis

By definition, a psychosis is a severe mental disorder in which thought, and emotions are so impaired that contact is lost with external reality. Someone can experience psychosis as a result of a mental illness. Also, it could be caused by a different health condition such as medication or from using drugs.

For the purpose of this chapter, we will go with information from *The National Alliance on Mental Illness* as well as some of my own experience with psychosis. It is from my experience that a psychological psychosis can be very taxing on the brain. It can be extremely hard to understand what is going on. In the United States alone, around one hundred thousand young adults will experience a psychosis annually.

It is important to get mental health care during the early signs of the development of a psychosis; this can be life changing and lifesaving. There are many early warning signs of a psychosis. A person may change their thoughts or perceptions gradually. Another sign can be a change in grades at school or decline in job performance. A person who is experiencing a psychosis can also have trouble thinking clearly or may find it hard to concentrate.

Another warning sign of an emerging psychosis could be a decline in a person's self-care or the way they would typically practice hygiene. A person experiencing a psychosis may also want more time alone. Lastly, an early warning sign could be strong or inappropriate emotions. However, the person could be found having no emotion at all.

During a psychosis, a person could hear, see, taste or even believe things that are not real. A person may also have an unusual thought pattern. In some cases, a person can hallucinate. A person may hear voices, have strange sensations or have feelings that they cannot explain. A person's eyesight could be distorted, and they can often see things that are not there.

A person experiencing a psychosis could have delusions. A person may believe things that are irrational to others. A person may believe that they have special powers or are on a special mission. Religion can seek its way into a psychosis. A person may believe that they are God or Jesus.

During a psychosis, even trivial remarks or events can have more of a meaning. One simple thing that someone says can have a large meaning in the mind someone in the middle of psychosis. Something that is just a simple concept can take on a whole new meaning in the brain.

In some cases, a person may believe that forces outside of them are controlling their thoughts. It may be believed that their feelings are being controlled. Even someone's behavior can be thought to be controlled.

My experience with psychosis is very interesting. About two years ago, a doctor changed my medication abruptly. I had been on it for over five years. I was stable and I had a very good quality of life. Within weeks, my mental health declined.

Then I entered into a psychosis. I was hospitalized in a very nice hospital in south Florida. In the hospital, there was plenty of friendly staff members and everything was clean. My psychosis went away after fixing my medication. The weird part about my psychosis at the time was that I believed that the United States was in the middle of a pandemic. Keep in mind, this was a year before we were hit with the corona virus pandemic.

During my psychosis, every pill I took, I thought they were different treatments for the outbreak. Every person, place or thing I cam across, entered my psychosis in their own way. The best way to describe it is that it was like there was a movie playing out in my head. The psychosis was like a movie being directed.

In my mind, I was an important part of the breakout puzzle. I felt a sense of importance that did not exist. This wasn't the first time that I had a psychosis like this. Anytime I've had a psychosis, there is always a catastrophe going on around me.

Typically, it is a pandemic or something ruining the world.

I don't typically see or hear anything that isn't there. Basically, my brain just makes a narrative of what is going on around me. Usually, my brain will resort to a worst-case scenario. Because of this when were hit with the corona virus pandemic, I was beside myself. It was like one of my episodes were playing out in real life.

According to *The National Alliance on Mental Illness*, people are still learning about how and why a person ends up developing a psychosis. Because of a change in the hormones in the brain, people at a young age can be more susceptible to experiencing a psychosis. This can be heightened during puberty.

There can be many causes for a psychosis including genetics, trauma, substance use, physical illness or surgery as well as mental health conditions. With genetics, a trait can either show up or lie dormant. Just because someone holds a gene that can lead to a psychosis, it doesn't mean that it will necessarily show up. There are ongoing studies on this to help us understand it better.

In my experience, bipolar disorder, depression and anxiety all run in my family. Mental illness is present in my maternal and paternal side. However, I never experienced a psychosis until I was twenty-four years old. It came on so fast and so strong. No one saw it coming until it was too late. I ended up in the emergency room and from there, an ambulance took me to a mental hospital.

Trauma can also be a cause for a psychosis. The type of trauma along with a person's age can impact how it may or may not trigger a psychosis. A traumatic event could be a death of a loved one or close friend, experience with war or even sexual assault.

If a person has an experience with psychosis, they can be more susceptible when using certain substances. According to *The National Alliance on Mental Illness*, the use of certain drugs like LSD, amphetamines and others can lead to a psychosis.

There are many ways to treat a psychosis. A family support team and education can go a long way. Typically, medication can be used as treatment of a psychosis. Psychotherapy can be a great tool in managing a psychosis as well. We can also seek support from our peers in group therapy.

9

Anxiety

According to *Psycom*, almost half of the people who have bipolar disorder will also be at a greater risk of experiencing an anxiety disorder. Sometimes, symptoms of anxiety disorders can even look like bipolar disorder symptoms. This can be yet another reason why getting a proper diagnosis. In this chapter, we will go over multiple types of anxiety disorders that can coincide with bipolar disorder such as:

- Panic disorder
- Generalized anxiety disorder
- Post-traumatic stress disorder
- Specific phobia
- Obsessive-compulsive disorder

When a type of anxiety occurs along with bipolar disorder, this is what psychologists refer to as comorbidity. I myself have bipolar disorder along with anxiety. I go more in depth about anxiety alone in *The Anxiety Warriors*, now available on *Audible*. I know how sometimes with anxiety; reading can be troublesome. Listening to *The Anxiety Warriors* may be easier.

First, let's go over panic attacks. These can occur in about twenty percent of people who have bipolar disorder. It can be more common in people who have mixed episodes and depression. There is an array of symptoms. Some physical symptoms of a panic attack include:

- Chest pain
- Heart palpitations
- Shortness of breath
- Dizziness
- Stomach aches

When someone has bipolar disorder, it can increase the chances of panic attacks. During a time when I was hospitalized back-to-back, I was experiencing high levels of anxiety. I was struggling with a few different major life changes. First, my family and I had just moved across the country. Also, I had a death in the family. During the week I was somewhat isolated where I lived. Lastly, I was struggling to pay for my medication.

I ended up having to be hospitalized after a medication change. After being released form the hospital, I found it challenging to maintain my stability. I found it hard to fall asleep. I ended up crying on my couch late at night with anxiety and panic.

Another type of anxiety that can be seen with people with bipolar disorder is generalized anxiety disorder. Besides panic disorders, this is the most common amongst people with bipolar disorder. With this disorder, someone will experience a constant state of worry. This state of worry will be excessive. This will happen almost every day for at least six months to be generalized anxiety disorder.

With this disorder, a person will worry excessively over things like personal health, interactions that occur socially and even from work or school. Symptoms of generalized anxiety disorder can include:

- Irritability
- Muscle tension
- Difficulty concentrating
- Disturbance in sleep
- Restlessness

It is interesting because some of these symptoms are the same as mania and depression. So, if we have bipolar disorder and generalized anxiety disorder at the same time, it may be hard to decipher which symptoms belong to which disorder. This is where a good working relationship with our medical team comes in.

Another anxiety disorder that can occur with bipolar disorder that can occur with bipolar disorder is social anxiety disorder. When it comes to this disorder, a person will have a self-conscious feeling in a social setting in extreme amounts. A person with this disorder can panic or can feel their mind going blank. Nausea and an increased heart rate can happen with social anxiety disorder.

Post-traumatic stress disorder can also occur in someone who has bipolar disorder. Many of us may have heard of this disorder. Post-traumatic stress can occur in people with bipolar disorder because manic and/or depression disorders can be traumatic. Post-traumatic stress disorder can be combined with a threat or even if physical harm has occurred.

There are many symptoms of post-traumatic stress disorder. These symptoms can include:

- Hostility
- Hypervigilance
- Mistrust in others
- Isolation
- Flashbacks
- Insomnia
- Nightmares

I understand how this disorder can occur along with bipolar disorder. I have had traumatic experiences with mania as well as depression. Also, I have ended up in some scary places due to my illness just as I have been in really great places. Sadly, it can make a difference in having good insurance versus having bad or no insurance in the treatment sometimes.

I have found it very hard to sleep in certain places. With some hospitals I have stayed, male and female patients sleep in the same area. This has made me uneasy, possibly because I am a victim of rape. I am not sure why I find this one so hard to deal with. In different hospitals, the male and female patients are separated, and it seemed a lot safer. However, as a patient, I still missed the comforts of home and it can be a grueling experience.

When we experience manic or depressive episodes, many aspects can be very traumatic. This can trigger even more anxiety. Another type of anxiety can be a specific phobia. I go over phobias in more detail in *THE MIND*, also available on *audible* and *amazon kindle*. It is interesting to learn that ten percent of people with bipolar disorder may also have a specific phobia.

Women are more likely to have a phobia than men. When someone has a phobia, it can be defined as having an extreme fear or aversion to a person, place or thing. This can be psychologically or physically disabling. This can be combined with bipolar disorder and often begins in childhood.

The last anxiety disorder that can occur alongside of bipolar disorder is obsessive compulsive disorder. This anxiety disorder can likely show up during a manic or depressive episode. A person with obsessive compulsive disorder will have repetitive, unwanted thoughts.

Because of the unwanted thoughts, a person may perform repetitive behaviors such as cleaning, counting, or washing hands. These repeated actions can occur in hopes that the recurring thoughts will go away.

Those of us with anxiety can help our disorder with an array of self-care. There are many relaxation techniques such as deep breathing, meditation, yoga and many other exercises that we can use to reduce stress. We will want to practice stress management such as getting into an activity we enjoy.

It is important to vocalize our problems in order to reduce stress. It is important to speak to a therapist, medical doctor or psychiatrist about our anxiety. In some cases, a medicinal therapy may be needed for a specific anxiety disorder.

10

Alcohol

Almost half of the people who have bipolar disorder have an addiction to alcohol. Treatment for alcohol addiction can vary depending on whether someone shows signs of having bipolar disorder before having a drinking problem or after. For the purpose of this chapter, we will go with information from *Healthline* as well as the *Mayo Clinic*. Also, we will draw from some of my personal experience.

When someone is in mania, this can increase the chances of risky behavior. Often times, drinking can be considered a risky behavior. Also, during a depressive episode, a person may turn to alcohol. The link between bipolar disorder and alcoholism isn't completely understood according to the information from the *Mayo Clinic*. However, genetics could play a role.

Those of us who have bipolar disorder have a clear difference in brain chemistry. This trait can have an impact on the way our brains react to drugs and alcohol. Some people with bipolar disorder may drink to deal with the depression symptoms and even to help with anxiety. However, doing this will have a negative consequence in the long run. Over time, drinking alcohol can exasperate the symptoms of bipolar disorder.

Drinking alcohol can increase mood swings, depression, violence and even chances of suicide. I have actually lost two family members who chose to mix alcohol with psychiatric medication. Both instances occurred near water. Therefore, it was unclear whether their deaths were accidental or suicide.

For people who have lost control over alcohol, it is important to seek help from a medical professional right away. Often times, bipolar disorder and alcoholism will get treated separately. However, a recent trend is to treat the two disorders at the same time. Medications and therapies can be used to treat bipolar disorder among with alcoholism.

For people who suffer from alcoholism, there is a twelve-step program. For many people, it isn't just a plan for becoming alcohol free, but it is used as a guide on how to live life. Now we will go through the twelve steps:

Step 1: Honesty: This can begin with simply admitting to being powerless over alcohol. This can occur after many years of being in denial.

Step 2: Faith: Having faith in a higher power can help one to overcome an alcohol addiction. In order for the effects of a higher power to work, a person must believe it can.

Step 3: Surrender: This step seems to be connected to step two. This step consists of turning our problems to a higher power.

Step 4: Soul searching: This step explains that going through recovery is more of a process than an event.

Step 5: Integrity: This step

involves a great amount of growth and can prove to be one of the more difficult ones.

Step 6: Acceptance: This involves a lot of letting go. We can accept that each of us have character flaws.

Step 7: Humility: This is where we will ask our higher power to help achieve something or give us a willpower to overcome an obstacle. Also, can simply ask for determination.

Step 8: Willingness: This is where someone will make a list of people they may have hurt before reaching recovery. A person will become willing to make amends with people.

Step 9: Forgiveness: This step is all about making amends. According to *Healthline*, this can be a bitter pill to swallow. However, this can be great medicine of the spirit and soul.

Step 10: Maintenance: This is where we can admit to being wrong. Many people may not want to admit to it, but it is how one will make progress in recovery.

Step 11: Contact: This is where we will find the path that is right for us.

Step 12: Service: This is where one can carry the message to others and to put the principles of the twelve-step program into practice in every area of life.

I myself battled with alcohol abuse in the past. I started using alcohol as a means to fall asleep at night. This was long before I discovered things like chamomile tea and melatonin. I started off by drinking a glass of wine a night. Then it would turn into two or three glasses.

At the time, I was only taking an antipsychotic medication. Also, this was before I got diagnosed with an anxiety disorder. The manic part of

my bipolar disorder is what prevents
me falling asleep. However, buying
alcohol to aid in sleep can be
expensive and unhealthy.

Luckily, for me, I was able to
break the cycle of drinking wine or
beer nightly. I was put on a mood
stabilizer to help with my fluctuating
moods with bipolar disorder. Also, I
was given an anti-anxiety medication
that also helped with sleep.

Now, I feel like I have a
healthy relationship with alcohol.
Once in a great while, I may enjoy a
glass of wine. I have noticed an
increase in the pressure to drink
around the holidays. If I am feeling

more on the manic side, I may give in to the pressure.

This is where we can turn to a therapist or a doctor for help. Also, we can ask friends and family for help. We can ask our loved ones and friends to keep an eye out for any problems with drinking.

Just like bipolar disorder, an alcohol addiction can be bigger than the individual. It may be difficult, but we must reach out for help when a problem is bigger than us. There are group therapies in person as well as online.

I have noticed that there can be a lot of pressure when it comes to alcohol besides the holidays. At many events with friends and family, people will nonchalantly offer me a drink. I have learned to confidently decline offers for drinks. At first some people will be offput. If a person values you and a decision not to drink, this will not be a problem.

If a person requires you to drink to be in their life, it may be time to set some boundaries. If the problem persists, it may be time to rethink the relationship. There have been numerous times where I have been offered an alcoholic beverage and I have declined. I have gotten an array of reactions. To some people, drinking alcohol may not be a big deal. However, for those of us with bipolar disorder, the ramifications can be high. We could trigger a mood swing or even an episode if we are not careful.

11

Self-Care

What does self-care look like for those of us with bipolar disorder? Well, it depends on what phase we are in within our diagnosis. Also, self-care can be different whether we are feeling hypomanic, manic, depressed, or having a mixed episode. Through trial and error, I have learned that keeping a daily routine can work wonders when it comes to having bipolar disorder.

First, we will want to wake up at the same time each day. I set my alarm for the same time each day. This is because I begin my workday as an author early on in the day. However, any time is good for waking up depending on what time we go to sleep. One piece of advice I've gotten is to fall asleep the same day you wake up. This may seem like simple advice but if I miss a night of sleep, I will end up in a bad place mentally.

I have found that if I skip a night of sleep, it all goes downhill from there. Because I sometimes have a hard time falling asleep at night, I make sure to wake up early and stay active throughout the day. Setting goals for self-care can be so important. When we take care of ourselves, our mood will be better and in turn, our illness will not take over our lives.

Now that I have been living with bipolar disorder for over ten years, I have discovered many ways to use self-care to my benefit. Self-care hasn't always been easy. As a wife, mother and author, it can be challenging to get all of the self-care needed.

Along with getting enough rest, we will want to work hard on hygiene. Getting clean should be a priority. I have found that the best time to work on hygiene is when I am feeling good. I will get a shower in wither before or after working or when I am feeling more energetic. Also, I will work on dental hygiene soon after dinner.

Some of us with bipolar disorder struggle with even getting out of bed sometimes. On those days, self-care could take a whole day; and that's okay. There is nothing wrong with having a day of relaxation and self-care. We want to keep our environment clean and comfortable so that our self-care can be easy. I also make sure to stock up on self-care items.

A good way to take care of

ourselves is by learning more. The more we learn about bipolar disorder, the better we will be able to manage our symptoms. There is a lot of information available online as well as in bookstores and libraries. Also, there are support groups that we can attend in person or online.

I have joined groups revolving around mental health and bipolar disorder. When I first joined, it was comforting to see that there were thousands of people like me who battle with bipolar disorder and other mental illnesses. Many people share feelings and dilemmas, making me feel less alone. I ended up starting my own groups on *Facebook*.

In addition to the online groups, I have attended an in person meeting for those of us with bipolar disorder. I was new so I took a seat at the end of the table. I was very nervous to talk. I sat patiently and listened to each person talk. Once it was my turn to speak, I already felt better about my disorder.

It became clear to me that many people go through similar trials that I go through with having bipolar disorder. At the time I attended my first in-person meeting, I was finishing up a master's degree in psychology. Since that day, I have battled with bipolar disorder in various ways. However, through self-care and a routine, I have managed to live a productive life.

Another area of self-care is having a work-life balance. Many of us with bipolar disorder work part-time or full-time and/or take care of household, children or even pets. Because of this, we may find it hard to get in the important self-care that we need. We will want to carve out time for healthy eating and getting in vitamins. Also, we want to maintain a certain level of fitness.

With all of our responsibilities, we want to make sure that we are putting our health first. We want to make sure that we are getting enough relaxation in. There are many relaxing activities such as writing in a journal, coloring, painting, and playing video games. We want to find a healthy escape from the stress of everyday life.

One thing those if us with bipolar disorder will get good at is problem solving. We will need to create healthy ways to manage our condition. Often times, a major life change will happen, and I will be blindsided by the consequence. Having a healthy self-care routine can really aid in battling changes and stress.

Here is a sample of a daily routine full of self-care:

6:30 a.m. Wake up, have coffee, and start the workday.

7:30 a.m. Have a healthy breakfast such as a smoothie or avocado toast.

8:30 a.m. Continue to workday.

10:30 a.m. Exercise either at home or at a gym.

12:30 p.m. Have a healthy lunch such as a salad and a bowl of soup.

1:30 p.m. Prep food for dinner

and clean.

2:30 Relax and read with a healthy snack such as almonds and apples.

3:30 p.m. Work on tasks (for me this could include writing a chapter, working with narrators or making a schedule).

5:30 p.m. Make or prep a healthy dinner.

6:30 p.m. Eat dinner with family without distractions.

7:30: Clean up and practice self-care such as showering and dental hygiene.

8:30 p.m. Read, watch

television or play a game.

I try to limit stress towards the end of the night. I will limit social media as the day comes to a close. I will take this time to chat with family and friends. At dinner time, we eat as a family without technology. However, we might pause and look up information about a subject we are talking about.

A big part of self-care is staying hydrated throughout the day. We will want to drink plenty of water or unsweetened decaffeinated tea. Also, almond or coconut milk is great as well. With some medications, I found that drinks with sugar become

more satisfying. However, in my case,
eating and drinking a lot of sugar can
lead to unhealthy weight gain.

12

Marriage

For about as long as I have had bipolar disorder, I have been married. I often question how we have been together over a decade despite my mental illness. A good thing to note, as my husband and I often do, is that there is no perfect person or perfect marriage. Every person has problems and so does every marriage.

I can still remember our wedding day like it was yesterday. I had a perfect ball-gown dress. My hair was done just so. I had my family and friends surrounding us. As my dad walked me down the aisle with a song I picked out towards the pier on the beach, I knew I was making the right decision.

As I walked up to my husband, I had to fight back my tears. We had gone through a lot to get to our wedding day. We were actually supposed to get married the year prior. However, I had my first brush with mental illness the year before.

With our wedding only about a month and a half away, I found myself at the mercy of mental health care workers. My then fiancé would bring me food, clothing and pictures

• • •

from home. He was as confused as I was as to what was going on.

Fast forward a year later, we were finally getting married. The pastor who married us had to fight back tears as he read our marriage vows. He had seen what we had gone through to get to our wedding day.

At the time of our wedding day, we were in an interesting situation. Due to my deep depression, I had asked if we could stay with my in-laws. I found it extremely difficult to be alone while my fiancé was working and at school all day.

My in-laws had a full house at the time. However, they offered to convert their dining room into a bedroom for us. I agreed and that was our living situation on our wedding day.

When we first moved in with my in-laws, I was in poor shape mentally. I had dropped out of college and lost my job. I couldn't see any hope for the future. But for some reason, moving in with family seemed to be an answer.

On our wedding day, I was in a great place mentally. Once we said, "I do" and kissed, it felt like a dream come true. Over the ocean and in front of our family and friends, we vowed to be together forever. After that, we went down to the beach and took pictures. The night finished with food and dancing.

In my mind, I had felt that all of our problems were behind us. On our wedding night, we kept our wedding clothing on as we walked along the beach sidewalks. Strangers clapped and cheered for us. We came upon a couple who congratulated us. They also said that the most important part of marriage was communication.

The longer we have been married, the more I realized that the couple we spoke to was right. Many times, our problems are solved through communication. When either of us have a problem, we wit down and talk about our children, finances, hope, dreams and fears.

Sometimes, one of us will have a problem with the other one's behavior. At first in marriage, this bothered me. Communicating about anything from parenting to finances was troublesome for me. Oftentimes, I would lash out in anger. I was so used to doing things my own way that it proved difficult to share every aspect of my life with another person.

I would like to say its luck that my husband and I have been married for over ten years. However, it has been a lot of work. We have fought through a lot of really bad days and hard times. My husband has seen me hypomanic, manic, depressed and deeply depressed.

It's hard to incorporate bipolar disorder into a marriage because of the unpredictability. Sometimes I don't know how I will feel in the morning. I could be on a great schedule of getting up early and working. Then, I will get blindsided by a spell of depression and my whole schedule can get thrown off.

As hard as I try to remain consistent as a person, I realize that this may never happen. Sometimes, life will be going perfect and then I can get hypomanic. IF left untreated, this can soon turn into mania and I will end up having to be hospitalized. This is not only hard for me, but I feel like it can be taxing on my marriage.

Even after a hospitalization, I will have a lot of work to do to reach stability. During this time, I will find myself questioning why my husband stays with me through all of the hard times. But he assures me that the hard times don't last that long and that the good outweighs the bad.

The truth is, as I navigate through marriage and bipolar disorder, all we can do is our best. Some days, I will need more sleep than others. Other days, I will need to order food versus cook. Some days I am very productive and other days it will take hours just to practice self-care.

In my opinion, we have built a very nice life together. Fast forward from our days of living in a dining room on our wedding day and now we have a two-story home, two children and a pet. My husband worked through college during our marriage and is now an engineer. I got back in school and earned a bachelor's degree.

After my first brush with mental health issues, I wanted to get a degree in psychology. My husband stuck by my side as I earned my master's degree in psychology. We both faced a lot of challenges together aside from me having bipolar disorder.

My advice for someone with bipolar disorder who plans to get married or who is already married is to put in the work. We must put in work to fight against our symptoms. It is important to follow the advice of our doctor and medical health team. We need to make sure that we are getting enough sleep. Also, we need to make sure that we take time for proper nutrition, self-care, and exercise.

Some people who have bipolar disorder may even choose not to get married or to end a marriage. This does not mean failure or that someone who is married is better off. Marriage can be hard and can take a lot of work. As me father puts it: "Being married is hard and being single is hard." I feel that he couldn't be more right. Next, we will dive into life as a parent combined with bipolar disorder.

13

Parenting

Two of the best days of my life were the days that my two children were born. I try not to take for granted the fact that I get to be a parent. However, some days with parenting can be harder than others. As parents, we stress out over many aspects of our child's life and their future. We want to give our children the best life that we can.

For those of us who have a mental illness, we may find ourselves worrying about passing our genetics down to our children. This is a legitimate concern. Before I became a parent, I had not been diagnosed with a mental illness. However, mental illness ran in my family. I inherited bipolar disorder from my father, but I don't blame him for my illness. I am grateful to be on the planet despite my disorder.

There are aspects of parenting that can be difficult with or without having a mental illness. Here are my top ten advice points for being a parent while having bipolar disorder:

- Make a schedule.
- Make time for self-care.
- Find activities for the

whole family.

- Plan meals and snacks.

- Plan for down time.

- Reach out for help when needed.

- Save money for activities and growth spurts.

- Practice healthy stress relief.

- Set boundaries.

One thing that has saved me with having children is making and sticking to a schedule. My children know what to expect each day. Breakfast, lunch and dinner are consistent. Between my husband and I, we will have the same activities at the same time each day.

Almost as important as having a schedule, is getting in self-care. Many of us have heard or seen the quote: "You can't pour from an empty cup." This couldn't be truer. We must figure out what we need and find a way to get it. My number one need for self-care would be getting clean. If I feel like I need a shower and can't get one, this can be a trigger for me.

I make sure to keep getting clean a priority. We can wake up early to practice self-care or schedule it in while our children are at school. Also, I go to a gym that has childcare. I can drop off my children and while they play, I can get a shower at the gym if need be. When my first sone was a baby, I would bring his chair into the bathroom while I showered. However, once he reached the toddler years, this wasn't feasible. I then would have to practice self-care during naptime.

It is important to try and do activities as a family. When it comes to technology, we will all use it at the same time. Then, after a certain amount of time, we will go technology-free. At this time, we can go for a walk as a family, go to the gym or even sit down for a game. We try to find activities for the entire family such as swimming or going to a park.

One thing that has really saved me, is planning meals and snacks. During the time that both of my children were toddlers, I would bring snacks and drinks with me if we were going out for a while. We can't always predict when our child will get hungry so we can try and plan ahead. My oldest child loves fruit salads so I will keep fresh fruit to cut up for him when he gets hungry. My youngest really enjoys cut up cheese with crackers so I will keep that on hand as well.

I like to plan down time for the

whole family. For instance, when my oldest child is out of school and my husband and I are off work, we may all relax for an hour or so. This can be a great time to use technology or read books. Also, before bedtime each night, we will have some downtime as well. This is when we will read books together. On a weekend, we might watch a movie as a family.

We don't always take advantage, but sometimes, we need help. It can be hard to practice parenting all of the time. Even the best parents need a break. We can reach out to family and friends to watch our children if we need a break.

If I need some time to work or practice self-care, I will let my husband know.

One area I go over in my other books is finances. For some of us, this may be a tough subject. We always want to be sure to have money especially for our children. It can be normal to feel inadequate in this area. I keep a savings account for each of my children. Each time I get a paycheck, I will put a small amount in each account. This way, if either child needs something, I will have the funds available.

When one of my children have a birthday coming up, I may put a little extra in their account. These accounts come in handy in case one of my children need new clothes because they grew. Also, they often need new shoes. Along with their savings accounts, I have an automatic deduction come out for their college accounts as well. A good suggestion would be to have a healthcare savings plan as well for each child. There can be quite a lot of doctor and dentist visits for young children. Also, before we knew it, it was time for my oldest to get braces. Any little bit we can save while our children are young can come in handy.

Just like work and daily life

challenges, parenting can add a lot of stress. Even though I swear I have two of the most perfect children, there can be stress involved. Now that my children are beyond the toddler years, I feel like there is a lot more breathing room. Before I used to have the stress of formula or changing diapers. Now, I worry if they are getting enough fruits and vegetables and if they are doing good in school.

Stress relief can look different for each of us as parents. We want to find healthy ways to manage stress. We will want to shy away from alcohol or drugs as a form of stress relief. This will only hurt in the long run. Having an alcohol or drug addiction along with bipolar disorder can be hard to treat.

Lastly, we will need to set boundaries as a parent. This can be in the form of saying no. At some points, our children may demand more from us than we are able to give. My husband and I have carried a screaming toddler having a tantrum out of a store or restaurant a few times. It is good to know that we can have boundaries and still be awesome parents!

14

Working

Working has always been important to me. From age twelve, I was interested in earning money. I made signs and hung them up all over the neighborhood . I had started my own lawncare business. Within days, I had clients lined up. I enjoyed waking up each day to work. I would take the money I earned and buy gifts for family and friends and use it one food and entertainment.

From there, I worked at a grocery store and then fast-food

restaurants. I also worked at a gas station and even a golf course. All throughout my college career, I worked to support myself. At age eighteen, my sister and I moved out to live on our own. It was then that I realized how expensive the world really was. I learned about electric bills and how expensive household items could be. In the past, I had worked two jobs at once while going to school. I would clock out at one job, change clothing, then go to the other job.

I didn't always work out of passion but out of necessity. I needed to buy things like gas and food. As I excelled in my college degrees, my work got more exciting and challenging. During my bachelor's degree, I was able to work with patients who suffered from various mental health conditions. I would be lying if I said that I didn't feel bad for all of the patients.

Every time I went to work, I wanted to rescue the patients. I watched one day as a doctor bought pizza for all of the patients in a mental health facility. In that moment, he might have offered an escape from the reality that the patients faced. There in the assisted living facility, they were not allowed to come and go as they pleased. There they stayed at the mercy of the staff and medical personnel like me who came and went.

Some of the patients that we faced were easier than others. One day, the doctor I worked for and I ended up in a place that was in very poor shape. A lot of the assisted living facilities we found ourselves in were older homes in Miami, Florida which were converted to care for patients. While the weather may have been nice, I could not have imagined being in some of the places we went to.

On this particular day, we were directed out to an old garage to do our work with the patients. All alone, was a woman in her mid-fifties. She was sitting in the dark smoking cigarettes. At the time, I was about five months pregnant. I had kindly asked the woman to put out her cigarettes so we could do our work.

All of the sudden, because I asked this of her, I became targeted. She started calling me names and badgering me. I will never forget, she kept calling me, "the cat's meow." She kept repeating it and it has always stuck in my mind. I never got mad about it. Rather I was intrigued by her behavior. I wanted to know why she kept saying that to me.

Another day with the doctor, we came across another run-down facility. We found ourselves in a small room with a couple of patients. All of the sudden, a man stood up and got in my face. He started screaming at me and using profanity. The doctor jumped up between me and the large man. Luckily for us, the man backed down.

Again, instead of being afraid or backing down, I was curious. I wanted to know why he did that. I wanted to get to know him. We continued our work and the man ended up being grateful.

There was another facility that

stuck out in my mind heavily. A man was standing at a table. He had a large head of frizzy brown hair. He didn't talk or move around much. However, he was drawing a circle over and over in a notepad. Again, I wasn't frightened, I wanted to know more.

Unfortunately, I was a mere medical assistant at the time. This was well before I had even thought about getting a master's degree in psychology. However, it was part of my journey. At this same facility, a man walked up to me. He was slightly shorter than me with a muscular build. He proclaimed, "I have people living in my body." I am still curious about that man to this day.

Once I started my master's degree in psychology, I knew I had found a home. Since then, I worked as a health coach and also a neurologist's office. Those were by far my two favorite jobs. At the neurologist's office, I was able to speak to people from all walks of life.

This chapter would not be complete if I didn't add how having bipolar disorder effects my ability to work. When I was first diagnosed, I didn't realize the impact having a mental disorder would have on my work life. Before my diagnosis, I had a completely sound mind. I could work two jobs, go to school, study and still have time for a social life. However, once I relapsed for the first time, I realized how fragile the mind can really be.

All of the sudden, I was taken back by medication times and doctor visits. Upon going back to work, I found it to be challenging with my new mindset. For a couple of years after my diagnosis, I battled with work-life balance.

Now, I have found a healthy work schedule. Working is now a big part of my life. I am able to schedule in self-care, exercise and nutrition along with my work schedule. Some days are definitely easier than others when it comes to work. I have learned to plan ahead and also take it day by day.

A Note from the

Author

It is possible to live a full life while having bipolar disorder. As someone who has this disorder, I have learned to change the way I do things. I can focus on the positive attributes of my personality to survive and thrive through life. Being a spouse, parent and author brings new challenges to my life every day. As humans, we all face different challenges. However, if we hone in on our intelligence and skills, we can get through our hardships. Thriving with

bipolar disorder will not always be
easy but it will always be worth it!

Feel free to find me on various
social media platforms:

Instagram: @avidauthor

Twitter: @psychologyamy

Facebook groups:

Psychology Facts

I Love Books

&

Mental Health Encouragement

Bipolar Disorder: Thriving, Triggers, Love & Relationships (Preview)

Amy Perez MS Psychology

Amy Perez

MS

Psychology

Introduction

Bipolar disorder is not the end
of the world. There I said it. It is not
who you are. It is part of who you are.
We are no different than someone
with high blood pressure or diabetes.
In the same way a person with
diabetes would check their blood
sugar, eat healthy and exercise, those
of us with bipolar disorder can keep
up a healthy mental and physical
lifestyle. It is highly possible to live a
happy, productive life while also
having bipolar disorder.

The reason I know this is because I lead one. I am a wife and a mother. I own a pet and take care of a household. I have a bachelor's degree and a master's degree. I have worked with underprivileged people living with various mental health issues. Lastly, I am an author of various mental health books. Do I have lows? Yes. Do I have highs? Absolutely. But just like checking my blood sugar, I check in with my moods throughout the day. Bipolar disorder is a mood disorder after all.

Am I feeling low? Why? Am I too energetic for no reason? It does take work, but it can be manageable. I have an arsenal of tools from nutritional factors to psychological factors. I also have certain family and friends to rely on in a time of need or crisis. Also, I keep a close working relationship with my doctor. This book breaks down the ten areas of anyone's life that are very important. But especially for us with bipolar disorder, it is important for us to keep track of our bodies and minds.

For anyone fresh out of the hospital or newly diagnosed, just take it slow. There is a lot to digest. And remember, I've been there. I was Baker Acted three times. Baker

Acted, for those who do not know is basically when you are held by law in a mental hospital. It is scary and taxing on your brain. I have tried and failed many times with medication. I have gone off of my meds thinking that I didn't need them. I have been suicidal. I have battled with self-medication with drugs and alcohol. I have sabotaged relationships from bipolar disorder rages. I have made poor sexual and financial decisions from hypomania, mania and depression. Does any of that sound familiar?

If so, you are in the right place. If you are a loved one of someone with bipolar disorder, guess what? So am I. So, it looks like we have a few things in common. My Master's degree is in Psychology and my bachelor's degree is in Nutrition. I was diagnosed with bipolar disorder in 2010. I have been hospital free for over six years. I have lived with bipolar disorder in my family since birth.

The encouraging news is that those of us with bipolar disorder can live well and be in society as productive members. We don't have to hide ourselves. It is okay to have a mental illness. I see my psychiatrist regularly and I take my medication daily. My loved ones and close friends are all aware of my illness. I openly talk about how I am feeling. I share my feelings and the people close to me share theirs too. I am happy to share with you as well!

Those of us with bipolar disorder can embrace our diagnosis and help support each other. We are all in this together. Life can be difficult. Just managing basic tasks like showering and cooking can feel like climbing a mountain. But we can thrive just as much as anyone else can. These ten areas of my life are very important. Each one of them can be problematic for those of us with bipolar disorder. And that's okay. We are learning and growing every day!

Money

You may be curious why I decided to start with money. Well, we all need money to survive. We have to buy food, pay bills, buy clothing and entertainment. For some of us, not all of our medication is covered by insurance. Therefore, money becomes especially important for someone with bipolar disorder. It is very easy to get caught up in hypomania or just extra excitement and overspend. It can be hard to stick to a budget or even make a budget.

Two years ago, I went to pick up my medicine from the pharmacy expecting to pay no more than fifteen dollars. My total for my medication that I needed was three hundred dollars. There was a gap in my insurance, and I wasn't covered for the full amount. I found myself at the mercy of family to get the medication I needed. I didn't have an emergency fund set up. I was not prepared for an extra expense.

On the extreme end, credit cards in the middle of a mall can be catastrophic. For me, the holidays can trigger me, and I will overspend. Those of us with bipolar disorder can get into serious debt with credit cards. For me, excessive shopping and financial hiccups can be a sign that I'm feeling manic. This can be a queue for me to open up to my husband and tell him how I'm feeling. A doctor appointment may be necessary.

However, I do pay my own bills and manage savings accounts. I do have credit cards, but my husband keeps them hidden. Anyone can battle with credit cards. I know that I will be triggered in a mall or with online shopping with my credit cards. I was open and honest about this problem area and now it is managed.

The lesson there is just being honest with yourself and others about how bipolar disorder can have a negative impact on finances. At the moment, I have cut up all of my credit cards except for two. It is good to find someone you can trust to at least be aware of your spending and to help give you advice. If you find that this problem area is over your head, make sure you speak to a doctor or counselor. Impulse control can be an issue and gambling could also be an issue. There are gambling hotlines in different states and cities that can help with that separately.

There are ways that those of us with bipolar disorder can handle money on our own. I have seen loved ones struggle in this area. Also, in my online groups, this area can cause problems. Some people seem to have simply given up. There are ways to set up your accounts to be successful. Here is an example:

Checking: $500.00

Savings: $200.00

Emergency Fund: $300.00

Fun/Vacations: $120.00

Gifts: $75.00

Kids: $100.00

Roth IRA: $75.00

My money is broken down into categories. My basic needs such as medication, food, gas and beauty supplies come from my checking account. My savings account is set up for little things that come up. I may need to pay a little extra for medicine or have an unexpected car repair. I have myself covered for unexpected expenses. Every time I earn money whether it is a paycheck or a gift, I will split off about twenty percent in this account. Another ten percent will go into the rest of the accounts. If a holiday or birthday is coming up, I may add more money into my gift account.

The emergency fund is set up for job loss or something out of my control. The fun and vacations account are set up for a weekend treat like a carnival or maybe a manicure. The gift account is set up for when my loved ones and friends have birthdays and for Christmas. This account keeps me from overspending on gifts which is my trouble area. The account for my kids is set up for when they want to join a sport or take lessons. Also, if anyone goes through a growth spurt, I'm covered.

Finally, my Roth IRA is set up for my future. There can also be separate accounts for stocks and CDs as well. Many bank accounts allow up to six free accounts. If overspending is an issue, alerts can be set up through the bank account. If accounts go below a certain amount, alerts can be emailed to you or a designated person.

A more extreme measure to take, if this area is largely problematic is to keep larger sums of money in an account that doesn't have a debit card attached to it. A second person required to withdraw money can also be a good measure.

Typically, financial mistakes can be repaired. I found it to be helpful to just focus on the future instead of dwelling on the past when it comes to finances. There are many finance books available for free at local libraries.

Nutrition

This is one of my favorite subjects to talk about. Many of us with bipolar disorder can suffer weight gain from medication, bouts of depression or both. Until I got a reduction in medication, I was suffering from extreme food cravings. I literally could not stop eating fried food, chocolate and candy. I packed on thirty pounds in less than a year. It is possible to maintain a healthy weight and take medication. It does take some work and dedication.

I like to watch nutrition videos online, read health magazines and read nutrition books. Nutrition is a science, and it is always changing. What we eat can have an impact on our moods and some foods can even have a bad reaction to our medicine. For instance, for one of my pills, I cannot eat grapefruit or drink grapefruit juice. Isn't that interesting?

One area for those of us with bipolar disorder that can make nutrition difficult is impulse control. Anyone can see a commercial for a pizza and be driven to order some. Not all people with bipolar disorder will battle with impulse control but some people might. Depression could make it worse. On the flip side, during hypo mania or mania, appetite can be severely reduced or non-existent.

Depression can be a time when certain foods are appealing. For instance, cocoa can naturally uplift our mood. It is no wonder that sweets with chocolate can make us feel better. Food is a wonderful thing for anyone. We celebrate with loved ones with food, we go out to eat and eat for entertainment. Also, alcohol can be involved during these occasions.

This is worth mentioning because those of us with bipolar disorder don't need to suffer with alcoholism on top of our illness. If you feel this area is a problem for you, absolutely seek help. Alcohol may trigger bipolar disorder symptoms and react negatively with our medication. Make sure to ask your doctor if you are able to drink on your medication. I myself decided to heavily limit myself when it comes to alcohol. For me, it just isn't worth it. Alcohol is a depressant. The morning after having more than one drink, I will find myself feeling down.

With alcohol, I have found that my true loved ones and friends accept me for who I am. They are comfortable with the fact that I don't drink very much. If someone makes you feel like you need to drink to be in their life, maybe rethink the relationship with them. That would be a great place to set some boundaries which we will discuss later.

If I want to wind down with a drink at the end of the night, I will make an iced chamomile tea. Chamomile relaxes the body and mind naturally. When thinking about drinking alcohol to bring down manic symptoms, think about talking to your doctor first. Ask if it is okay to take melatonin supplements or they may prescribe you something different. Melatonin can be bought over the counter.

Another chemical of choice by many of us is caffeine. I love coffee. Coffee keeps me going especially as a parent and as an author. Sometimes I plan on sleeping until eight o'clock but wake up at five. So, yes caffeine plays a role in my life. However, too much caffeine can be bad for anyone. Caffeine can have an effect on the mood. The fact that bipolar disorder is a mood disorder makes this area important. Be careful with caffeine. Talk to your doctor about a safe amount for you.

I personally know how some medicine can make us tired and out of it. I make sure to rotate coffee with tea, juice and almond milk. Also, caffeine too late in the day can make it hard to sleep at night. Also, worth mentioning, a lot of caffeinated drinks contain a lot of sugar which can lead to weight gain. It seems like sugar is hidden everywhere. Make sure to read labels and keep track of sugar intake. Women can have twenty-five grams of sugar a day and men can have thirty-seven.

It is important for us with bipolar disorder to eat! We should eat whole foods and enjoy food. Cooking and learning new recipes can make us feel better. However, when we are feeling down or low on energy, it's a great idea to keep healthy and easy meals on hand. Also, have restaurants in mind that offer healthy options for when cooking isn't an option. Increasingly, there are more restaurants and grocery stores offering delivery options. These are great for planning ahead or last-minute meals.

Keeping fresh snacks like nuts, apples and bananas is a good idea too. I keep nuts and fruit in my purse and car at all times. It helps with stress from traffic and I find myself staying away from fast food more. These foods are good for us, help with mood and maintain a healthy weight. Keeping a schedule for eating is good too. Make sure to eat breakfast, lunch and dinner. Add two or three snacks in between. I make sure to eat a healthy snack when I take my medicine. I will do a yogurt and banana at night. Sometimes, medicine can upset our stomachs if we don't eat enough or eat the wrong thing. Make sure to check with your doctor about any foods that can react with your medicine.

Most importantly, enjoy food that you love! Two or three times a week, make sure to treat yourself with a favorite meal or snack. Go out with friends or loved ones and enjoy food. It is important for our mood to have a healthy relationship with food. Stay away from fad diets and don't limit your calories too much. We need our brains and bodies working at an optimal level. Starving ourselves is not the answer. Also, weight loss pills and supplements can have a bad reaction for us. Some of them contain high levels of caffeine or other harmful chemicals. It is important that we treat our bodies well because it impacts our brain and vice versa.

Here is an example of a typical daily meal plan with a medication schedule:

9:30 a.m. Breakfast

1 hard-boiled egg

1 cup of oatmeal

1 banana

1 glass of orange juice

1 cup of coffee

11:00 a.m. Snack

½ cup of almonds

1 apple

12:30 p.m. Lunch

1 black bean or chicken taco

1 side salad

1 cup of low-fat milk or almond milk

1 cookie

(Medicine)

3:30 p.m. Snack

Tea, coffee or juice

1 protein bar or oatmeal

6:00 p.m. Dinner

6 ounces of salmon

1 cup of broccoli

1 cup of mashed potatoes

9:30 p.m. Snack

Choose 2 or 3:

- Yogurt
- Berries
- Granola
- Popcorn
- Cheese

- Banana

(Medicine)

At night, I will have a snack with my medicine and read a book or listen to music. Sometimes, those of us with bipolar disorder have trouble falling asleep at night. We will talk about that soon.

On the weekend or on a date night, I will enjoy fried food or pizza. I get treats with the kids on occasion also. Nutrition does coincide with fitness which we will discuss next.